$\mathcal{M}$EDITATIONS *for* SELF-DISCOVERY

• *Guided Journeys for* •
Communicating with Your Inner Self

SHEPHERD HOODWIN

Summerjoy Press
NEW YORK
1995

Dedicated to my friend

Patricia Marie Englert

———＞•◉•＜———

Meditations for Self-Discovery—Guided Journeys for Communicating with Your Inner Self

Published by:
Summerjoy Press
FDR Station Box 7590
New York NY 10150-1913

Distributed by:
Atrium Publishers Group
Box 108
Lower Lake CA 95457
800-275-2606

Printed in the United States of America.

ISBN 1-885469-01-2
Library of Congress Catalog Card Number 94-092316

99 98 97 96 95

15 14 13 12 11 10 9 8 7 6 5 4 3 2 1

Cover design by Melody Cassen.
Photograph of Shepherd Hoodwin by Billy Jim.

CONTENTS

﹅ INTRODUCTION ﹅

These meditations were channeled from my essence (higher self) as part of the "Michael Speaks" lecture series in New York City to help draw the group together. Originally, they lasted about fifteen minutes each, including pauses and the concluding open-ended exploration, but they can be shorter or longer depending on the pacing. (The unguided segment allowed me to concentrate on bringing in the Michael entity, whom I channeled for the rest of the evening.)

You can use these meditations individually or in a group; many are suitable for discussion afterward. You can read them or play them on a cassette, with or without music—it can be valuable to record them in your own voice, and prerecorded cassettes may also become available (write the publisher for information).

I have omitted instructions about posture, closing and opening your eyes, etc. It is recommended that you keep both feet flat on the floor when you are sitting on a chair, or sit cross-legged, yoga-style. Keep your palms up, your back straight, and your head buoyantly elevated as if a string attached to your crown were drawing it upward. It is helpful to begin with a few moments of silence, consciously releasing any tension in your body, and stilling your mind. Listening to your breathing can help focus your concentration.

These meditations can provide vehicles for new experiences of energy and communication from your inner self. Let your imagination be free. Your imagination can operate through any of your senses, not just visually. Some people's imaginations are not particularly visual. Whatever ways in which you experience these meditations are valid. In this book, "to see" refers to the inner sight, however it operates in you, whether through vision, sensation, sound, or abstract thoughts and feelings.

If no images or sensations come to you, you don't need to "try," but you can make up something or "pretend" you're having the experience of the guided meditation until images and/or sensations come freely. Once they do, take your hand off the wheel, so to speak: let the experience come from within, without thinking. Let yourself be surprised by what comes up. There is space after each meditation to record your experience.

As with dreams, examining what your imagination brings to you is a potent way of learning about yourself. Some people are afraid to meditate because they do not wish to face what might come up from their subconscious. These meditations are designed to promote a positive experience; if something disturbing does comes up, no doubt it is something that needs your attention. The best approach is to objectively observe it, as if it were a movie, write it down afterward, and when you are ready, explore it, perhaps with a professional counselor of some kind.

If you read these meditation aloud, let your voice be warm and colorful, as if you were telling stories.

May they guide you into many wondrous adventures!

❧

1 ❧ THE GREAT MOTHER

I magine that you are in the midst of a magnificent, ancient forest. The air is so alive that it almost intoxicates you. Take a deep breath. Feel the oxygen enliven every part of your body. Imagine yourself now lying down on a soft bed of leaves and pine needles. Notice the rich scent in the air and hear the awesome stillness. The earth cradles you in her arms. You feel totally loved and protected by her. You feel her heart beating beneath you in her crystalline core.

As your body rests and is rejuvenated by her healing powers, your spirit takes wing and soars above the treetops. As far as the eye can see are beautiful trees of all kinds, snow-capped mountains in the distance, and a magnificent, brilliantly clear sky. The sun energizes your spirit and gives you a gift to take back with you to the Great Mother. Spend a moment becoming aware of what that gift is.

You are now ready to visit the Mother in her most secret place. You find yourself over a lovely, green hilltop that beckons you into it. You easily pass through its surface and float down until you find yourself in the very core of the earth. You have never seen such beautiful, crystalline formations, in shades of green, yellow, blue, and white that you had not before even imagined. This is the most beautiful place that you have ever seen. Take a moment and become fully comfortable there.

You are approached by another spirit. She is the Most High Priestess of the Great Mother. Her word is the word of the Mother herself. You embrace, and as you do, you feel totally one. You present her with the gift you have brought from the sun. The Most High Priestess invites you to enjoy this gift as it is given to the Great Mother. The gift is placed upon an incandescent silver plate. It rises from the place you are and disappears, but becomes an integral part of this place. Continue to enjoy the gift and your entire experience being in the heart of the Mother.

 **NOTES**

2 ❧ THE PRESENCE

Imagine the presence of a great warmth that feels utterly nurturing, good, and peaceful. See it as the most beautiful color or colors that you can imagine. If it is multicolored, notice its design.

Feel it as having the texture or sensation of something incredibly soft, like a favorite blanket or article of clothing, the skin of a baby, or the fur of an animal.

Imagine that you can smell this presence. Perhaps it is like lilacs, a forest after it has rained, or cookies baking.

You are utterly surrounded by the color, softness, and scent of this presence. It permeates every cell of your body, enlivening it. It is healing everything that is not well in your body. It is causing every muscle to release old, static energies. The energies of your body are now flowing beautifully.

This presence is calming your mind. The "bumps" are being smoothed as if by a gentle breeze blowing over them. You know that there is an answer to every question troubling you and that you are capable of knowing it. Feel your mind unwind, becoming still.

This presence is filling your emotions with balance and richness. Every troubled feeling is embraced in this presence and made whole.

This presence now pervades your entire spirit. Everything that moves out from you and comes in to you is full of the lovely color, softness, and scent of this presence. Something deep inside of you breathes a deep sigh of relief. You are home again. This presence is you.

❧

NOTES

3 ❧ GOOD RELATIONSHIP

See everything as being white, as if you were in the midst of the fluffiest, whitest clouds imaginable.

Ask within to be in good relationship with everyone in your life. Think of a few people individually and feel yourself being in good relationship with them. Feel these relationships growing and deepening.

Ask to be in good relationship with the sun, the moon, the stars, and the earth. Feel these relationships growing and deepening.

Ask to be in good relationship with yourself. Feel this relationship growing and deepening, including all aspects of yourself.

Ask to be in good relationship with the whole. Feel this ultimate relationship growing and deepening. Ask that you remain in good relationship with the whole as you return your awareness to the room.

NOTES

4 ❦ THE CRYSTAL CAVE

See yourself in a magnificent cave high in the Himalayan Mountains. This is no ordinary cave, but a cave whose walls are made of crystals of all kinds and colors. Facing you is a wall of clear quartz studded with diamonds and rubies. Behind you, the wall is rich aquamarine, yellow citrine, and tourmalines of all kinds around the border. This cave is light and dark at the same time. There is no sunlight but there is so much radiant energy coming from these beautiful minerals that it feels bright.

These energies enfold and envelop you. They are healing all your sadness, pain, and grief. Your anger, rage, and resentment are being transmuted into pure power, assurance, and strength. All your worries, heaviness, and difficulties fade away. You begin to know that whatever happens, you can handle it with ease and wisdom.

All distorted energies in your body are being drawn out through your feet into the floor of the cave and neutralized. You feel washed clean in its light. You feel completely one with all life in the universe.

Take a moment now and let yourself experience whatever you wish in this cave.

NOTES

5 ❧ JOURNEY THROUGH YOUR MIND

Check your body out. Be for a moment with any part of your body that is tense or blocked. Feel the barriers to freedom in that part of your body dissolving. Notice your breathing. Deliberately let it relax, so that it does what it naturally does without interference.

You are going to take a journey, a journey through your mind. You are comfortably seated on a magic flying carpet. It gently lifts you off the ground. You have perfect control. You can stop, move slowly or quickly, and otherwise go however you wish.

As you enter the chamber of your conscious awareness, first take a look at its landscape. Notice the colors, shapes, and overall impression. Ask that the magic carpet carry you to the thought form that most needs to be seen by you in clarity.

Be there now. Look at it. Do not analyze it. Just see it for what it is. Feel welling up in you a great compassion for this form, whether it is ugly or beautiful, misshapen or symmetrical, full of strife or peace. Know that it is there for a good reason, and that as you see it and work with it, it serves your growth perfectly.

As if with X-ray eyes, see the insides of this thought form. Feel a great sense of peace. Let the love from the depth of your being pour out and totally surround it. Watch how it changes as you do this.

When you are ready, move your carpet forward until you come back around in a circle to where you entered. Exit the chamber and have the carpet put you down safely on the ground.

 **NOTES**

6 ❧ HAPPINESS

Notice your emotions. What color or colors are they? What shapes do they make?

Notice your thoughts. Again, what colors are they? What shapes do they have?

Notice the energies of your physical body. Where are they moving? Where are they not? Try slightly adjusting the way that you are sitting and see if your energies move more freely in your body.

Notice how the planet feels, both the earth under your feet and the sky all around. What does the Great Mother, the earth itself, wish to say to you?

Go back now to your body. Find a place of tension in it that has something to say to you and ask what that is. When you are done, take a deep breath, let it out, and then take another. Let that tension go.

Remember a happy feeling from the past, or imagine one now. If you like, tie it to a scene or image. Feel the feeling. Be in the middle of it. Let the happiness of that feeling fill you full and overflow beyond you, filling the room. Imagine sharing it with loved ones, and receiving their happiness as well. Continue exploring this happiness. If it has a color and shape, see it; if it has movement, feel it. Ask it to open itself to you, so that you can be a part of it.

NOTES

7 ❧ THE SUN

Feel the atmosphere all around you. Sense how it vibrates. Is it peaceful? Is there some anxiety hanging around also? Discern whatever it is, without judgment.

Feel the sun brightly shining overhead, warming the atmosphere as if it were noon on the most perfect June day imaginable. Feel the earth underneath, green and rich, soaking up those golden rays of light, and reflecting back the radiation commingled with its own healing energies.

Feel the atmosphere all around you again. Notice if it has changed, and how, if it has.

Imagine that the core of the sun is comfortably warm, not hot. It is now in the middle of this room, and you are in the midst of it. How convenient it is to be able to get a tan on all parts of your body without having to turn over! You are relaxing as if you are lying on a magnificent beach hearing the crash of the waves against the shore, your body melting peacefully into the earth beneath you, totally supported, only the sun's light is coming from all directions. Your breathing now is deep and easy. It is lovely being in the midst of the sun! Be with that experience for a few moments. Notice what happens.

The sun is a perfect embodiment of love. Feel yourself basking in the glow of being totally loved. Feel that every part of your physical body is loved. Feel that every thought of your mind is loved. Feel that every feeling you have or you have ever had is loved. Feel that every spiritual dimension of your being is totally, completely loved.

Find yourself becoming increasingly one with the sun. The more that you receive its gracious blessings, the more you have them to give. Feel yourself becoming love, giving off the same golden rays that you have been receiving. Imagine everyone else as being included in the sun as well, a part of what you are.

 **NOTES**

8 ❧ VISITING VENUS

Feel your feet as though they were connected by means of magnetic rods to the core of the earth. Imagine what that core is like. Rising up from it through your feet is a substance as sweet and heavy as a July afternoon spent in a hammock under a shady elm tree. Feel the substance of the earth filling you all the way past the top of your head, giving you the greatest sense of well-being you have ever known. Allow yourself to feel completely nurtured by the earth. She is the Great Mother, and she loves you totally.

See her great friend, the moon, full and beautiful, hanging above you in the sky. Feel totally enveloped in her silvery light. As your body melts in this nurturing, feel yourself become lighter and lighter, more and more free. You begin to lift off the ground and float, higher and higher. You see a beautiful, gaseous planet ahead of you.

You are now in the atmosphere of Venus, the voluptuous Goddess of Love. Her air is more velvet-like than that of the most perfect twilight in June. Every breeze caresses you. You are like a child playing. Go off and explore. What do you find of Venus's hidden treasures? What colors surprise you? What new shades of lavender and pink do you find that you did not even know existed? What new flowers do you come across? Pick one and go inside it. Be that flower from within it; breathe in its magnificent scent; luxuriate in it.

Know that Venus, the Goddess of Love, is your friend. Know that you can have all that she has to give.

❧

Feel completely loved by her. This makes you so happy that you want to dance and turn somersaults in the air. Let yourself do that, or anything else that you wish to do in her glow. When you are ready, return to earth, bringing the energy of your friend with you.

 **NOTES**

9 ✿ LISTEN!

Listen. Listen to the beating of your heart. Feel the blood move in your veins. Sense the air against your skin. Know how perfectly your toenails fit with your toes. Be aware of how large your aura is. Understand that your body is a miracle.

Notice how quickly your thoughts move, faster than the speed of light. For instance, think how little time it takes between the time you decide to lift your finger and the time that it is lifted. Marvel at the speed.

Feel the richness of your emotional state. Feel all the feelings that are in you and around you. You contain a library of emotions from A to Z. Check out the one called joy and feel the joy that is present, awaiting to be experienced. Now go through the library and find other emotions that are like old friends to you: happiness, well-being, peace, excited anticipation, and anything else that you would like to check out. When you are ready, come back to the room.

❧ NOTES ❧

10 ❧ THE MATRIX

Imagine that there are invisible bonds connecting you to all people. You are an intersection in the beautiful, multicolored net of humankind. Imagine now that the net is becoming three-dimensional, slowly rising above you and falling below you, continuing to make grid patterns, until it includes every level of being in the universe.

Experience yourself as part of this great matrix. Feel how your energy begins to flow more freely when you feel connected to the larger pattern. Feel that no matter what you do, no matter where you go, you can draw upon this whole which is greater than the sum of its parts.

Imagine yourself leaving your body now as if on a retractable cord to explore other reaches of this whole. See yourself visiting a higher level of existence. Notice what colors you encounter, if any. Notice shapes, if any. You have great freedom of movement, so explore as freely as you would like.

Take flight again and visit the realm of the matrix below you, deep into the heart of the Great Mother herself. Feel her hospitality welcome you as you have never been before. Feel the lush textures of her enfolding grace. Smell the sweetness of the air like a perfect summer evening ten times over. Feel how at peace and at home you are.

Take a few moments now and explore any realm that you would like. You have the run of the universe. It is all part of this matrix. When you are ready, come back to the room and feel connected to all the places that you have visited.

 **NOTES**

11 ❧ THE MAGICAL WIND

Feel yourself surrounded by a magical wind. It does not just flow by in one direction; it spirals around you. It encircles you from your feet up, carrying away all cares, worries, and tensions past the top of your head, way up into the sky, like the smoke of a candle ascending to the heavens.

This wind has a sweet perfume about it. It smells of the richness of the earth: wet grass, lilacs, roses, and many other scents commingling, tantalizing your sense of smell.

Feel it pouring out of your insides, cleansing and cooling you, making you peaceful. As this process continues, feel it expanding in all directions around you, healing and drawing everything together in love.

Feel the wind now making you totally light. You are becoming a part of it. It lifts you up and sets you down in a beautiful, fluffy white cloud, as though you were being placed upon a throne. Look down from here and see the earth stretching for miles beneath you. See its rivers, its hills, its cities, and its forests. Feel pouring out of you the love of the wind for the earth. Feel yourself being the wind caressing its surfaces, moving easily and quickly over it.

Go to a specific place on the earth which needs your love, and give it. Spend as much time there as you choose. When you are ready, come back and be in your body as the wind.

NOTES

12 ❧ LOVE

Remember a moment when you felt totally loved. Ask that this memory surface from wherever it is stored in consciousness. Do not struggle to remember this feeling; instead, ask that it be given to you, and quietly receive it, fully expecting it to come to you.

Remember a time when you felt totally loving, either towards another person or towards the world in general, and let that feeling fill you.

Now, ask that both feelings join and blend. Feel this love permeating the domain of your daily work; feel it surrounding you in that situation, and feel it surrounding all those with whom you have contact during the course of a day. Individually surround the key people in this vibration. If you are not presently working, surround with love those that you have in your daily life in other ways.

See everyone in your personal life filled and surrounded with love. See every part of your physical body filled to overflowing with love. Extend this love to every thought of your mind, both those that are confused and those that are clear, those that are finished and those that are unfinished. Love every emotion: every element of anger, joy, resentment, appreciation, happiness, sadness, fear, and confidence. Surround them all in this vibration, accepting them and letting them be integrated into you. When you are done, be with the love vibration in its pure essence. When you are ready, come back to the room.

NOTES

13 ❦ VISITING THE CENTRAL STAR

As dusk approaches, the clear blue night sky becomes darker and darker. A bright star begins to appear, growing brighter and brighter. This is your star. See it and know it.

It draws you up into itself. It feels warm and cool at the same time, and you are wholly comfortable in it. From it, you see the earth as it sees the earth. This star is the central star of all the universes, far larger than our whole solar system. It is home to you. As you look around you, you see amazingly beautiful structures for dwelling, working, and playing, made up of colors so intense and vibrant that they cannot be described.

You see many of your old friends welcoming you back. They see how much you have changed and grown during your time on earth. You go to visit a great teacher whom you love and respect deeply. He has a message for you.[1] Sit now with him and talk with him. Receive his message. When you have fully received this message, complete your visit and come back into your body on earth, your home away from home, and see it with new eyes.

---

[1] The soul has no gender, but contains both the masculine and feminine. For convenience's sake, the words *he* and *his* refer to both male and female throughout this book. You may wish to substitute *he and she* and *his and her*, or simply *she* and *her*.

NOTES

I magine a peaceful, balmy place. Perhaps it is a grassy knoll beside a pond, or a cool, shady spot off a mountain trail. Maybe it is a thousand yards under the surface of the ocean where, by miracle of thought, you are able to breathe completely comfortably and see the beautiful coral and the fish swimming by as you sit on a rock. Maybe it is on the inside of a giant cloud where angels hang out, inviting you to lie on a lacy hammock woven from the cloud itself. Perhaps it is on another planet where you see things you have never seen before.

Wherever you choose, it is a place where you can think very clearly and with wisdom about yourself. Explore what you feel to be your highest reason for being on earth and lucidly evaluate how much you are satisfying that reason. Commit to doing one thing that will more deeply fulfill your reason for being here on earth. Do not be overly elaborate; choose something simple, something you can do now.

Do not analyze why you have not been doing it as much as you would like. Do not judge yourself. Simply choose. This choice is between you and yourself—no one else needs to know about it. It is chosen from your inner sanctum, your private, holy place. Protect that place and protect whatever you commit to when you are there.

NOTES

15 ❦ COLORS

I magine that you are in the midst of a ball of white light. This ball is soothing and healing to you. As it circles, it cleanses away all negative vibrations. As the light grows brighter, you feel yourself becoming more and more one with the light. You are the light.

Circling around this white light are many beautiful colors. See these colors around you now. They are your colors, the special colors that you bring in your life. As the white light washes through these colors, it cleans and brightens them.

Become aware now of one other person. Connect with his white light, and sense the beautiful colors around it. See his white light blend with yours, and watch your colors interact.

Now connect with the white light of all humanity. Imagine it as a giant ball, giving off colors which join together into one ever-changing dance of motion and shape, becoming more and more magnificent. Enjoy being in this collective light.

NOTES

16 ❧ THE ANGEL'S GIFT

Imagine that you are as light as air. Feel this lightness throughout your entire body, your mind, your emotions, and your spirit. You are so light that you can soar through the air or float like a cloud suspended in the sky. You are also light-filled, growing brighter and clearer in your radiance. In your mind's eye, look around you and see fellow light-beings. Notice how each is different, and yet the light is the same.

Now look up and see that a magnificent angel is coming to you. This is your favorite angel. Greet him and take his hand. He wishes to show you something. You effortlessly move with him to the special place where he takes you. You are there now. See now what it is that he wishes to show you. He gives you a gift, a priceless gift, to take back with you, something to share, something that can enrich the whole. Look it over. Get to know it. When you are ready, come back to the room, still feeling light, and share your gift in your heart with the whole, either directly or through someone who would especially benefit from it.

NOTES

17 ❧ THE ANGEL'S PERSPECTIVE

Envision yourself as you might be seen by an angel. Look down upon yourself with unfathomable compassion and fond regard. See the beautiful colors of your aura. See them slowly change. See the patterns that these colors make.

Know, as an angel would, how good your heart really is. Forgive yourself for all your mistakes, real and imagined. Relax completely under your loving gaze. Know that all the limitations of mind, emotion, and body are but your teachers. You no longer need feel guilty about them.

Go a little higher still and see your brothers and sisters as angels see them. Notice the superficiality of the boundaries separating you. See with love their short-comings. See their greatness, and be inspired by their beauty. When you are ready, come back to the room.

NOTES

18 ❧ THE REGATTA

You are on a boat floating down a river. The water is clear, and is the most beautiful shade of blue you have ever seen. On both sides of the river is a profusion of flowers, shrubs, and trees of many varieties. It is about five o'clock on a summer afternoon. The sky is cloudless. The sun warmly caresses your back.

Your boat is very special. It is made of different kinds of wood from all over the world. It is embedded with magnificent gems, and trimmed with gleaming gold and silver. As you lounge upon it, you are filled with its healing and strengthening powers.

From every direction, you are receiving beauty and nurturing. You are filled with a great sense of well-being.

Now the river opens into a harbor of a great sea. Here you see many of your friends on magical boats similar to yours. It is a heavenly regatta. All the boats are beginning to come into formation. The boats begin to leave the harbor together and enter the sea. In the sky above you, banners, balloons, and fireworks of all the colors of the rainbow appear. You are going on a joyous mission. All of you together are bringing to the world a demonstration and experience of being one in the Light. Stay with your boat; see where it leads you. When you are ready, sail it to an appropriate harbor and come back to the room.

NOTES

19 ❦ THE FOUNTAIN

I magine a spot on the floor through which is spraying a fountain of exquisite colored lights. These gem-like rays are cascading over and around you. Notice the colors and the patterns. This being a living fountain of light, it is constantly changing. Like a fireworks display, it sometimes surprises you in its formations. However, it is totally soothing. Enjoy it for a moment.

You are now as light as the light itself. You can play and interact with the rays of light as you wish. You can let yourself be suspended on the tip of the current. You can slide down the side of one of the rays. You can become one of them. Do whatever you wish to, improvising as if you were playing music with a band. Have great joy playing in this fountain.

NOTES

L et yourself be utterly relaxed. Allow each muscle of your body to fully let go.

Into all the myriad spaces in your body seeps a rich healing liquid. It is of whatever colors are to your highest good. Your body begins to take on a new glow, as if you were a kaleidoscope turned inside out. This spiritual liquid begins to exude from you and fill all the spaces in the room, creating a living stained-glass window through which a brilliant inspirational light shines upon the world.

The source of that light is in your heart. Be there now. Feel the light becoming brighter. Feel it continuing to heal your body. Receive it into your mind, your emotions, and your spirit. The liquid filling in the spaces inside and outside your body is a perfect magnifier of the light, like dew drops on a leaf, or fluid crystals. The light becomes stronger and stronger. This room is now like a kaleidoscopic lighthouse, sending forth a great light into the darkness.

Again bring your awareness to your heart. Be there. Feel the light. Be the light, and let it shine.

NOTES

21 ❧ SUNBATHING

Imagine that you are lying on your back, floating on an air mattress in the middle of a large, perfectly quiet swimming pool. It is one o'clock in the afternoon. The sky is clear. The sun is wonderfully warm on your skin. You haven't a care in the world. Every muscle is letting go. You easily absorb the sunlight and all that it has to offer you. Receive it. Feel its soothing heat in every part of your body. Feel it healing your body.

Imagine now that the sun is shining upon your mind. Receive its soothing warmth. Receive its light, wisdom, and understanding. Now receive the light and warmth of the sun into your emotional body, soothing your sadness, calming your anger, helping you feel connected to all being, helping you feel thoroughly loved.

Receive the sunlight into your spiritual body. Experience its cleansing. See your aura being filled with sunlight and beauty. Revel in it as you continue to lie on your back in the swimming pool filled with sparkling clear, healing water.

NOTES

Look into a pitch-black sky. It is absolutely quiet, except for the occasional musical sound of crickets chirping. The air is warm and soft on your skin. You are utterly comfortable, at home, and at peace. You lie down on soft, thick grass and gaze at the stars. How far is the farthest one? Perhaps a million billion light-years away? Or are you really looking into infinity? From this peaceful meadow, it feels like you can see forever.

Imagine what it might be like on a planet surrounding that farthest star. Maybe someone just like you is lying in a meadow looking at our star and thinking the same things that you are. Although you may not consciously know the life form he inhabits, you can sense that you and he are a part of the whole, and in spirit, are one. Become aware of this unmet friend who is perhaps a million billion light-years away, or perhaps could be said to be at the other end of infinity. Feel yourself drawing closer and closer to him until, as if by magic, he is in your meadow right beside you. You look upon him with great love and joy for having the wonderful opportunity to meet him in person. You look each other over and muse at one another's life forms. Then you link hearts—you feel each other's essences.

Take a couple of minutes now and get to know each other in this way. You cannot communicate in words, yet you both find it easy to know what the other is thinking and feeling. You know that you are rapidly becoming dear friends. After a few minutes, he will rematerialize in his native home and you will come back to the room, but you will not feel separate.

 **NOTES**

23 ❧ EARTH MUSIC

Listen. Listen deeply to the sounds of the earth. They are present underneath all outer sounds. Let your listening take your awareness thirty feet below the surface of the ground. You hear giggling. It makes you giggle, too. Be with this lighthearted, carefree energy. Feel its happiness coming into you.

Listening a little deeper, you hear the sound of beautiful singing. You have never heard such singing. Is it one voice or many? Feel the singing lifting your spirits, exalting you.

Listening deeper still, you hear a symphony, you might say the music of this sphere, earth music. It makes you want to dance, and within yourself, you do. Feel how free you are, how creative!

Let your listening now take you to the core of the earth, a place of many crystals. I will not describe its sound, because it is indescribable. Listen to it for as long as you wish, and when you are ready, come back to the room.

NOTES

24 ❧ BECOMING ENERGY

The molecules of your body are vibrating faster and faster, becoming less and less dense. Your body is becoming pure energy. In this energy body you can go anywhere instantly. Find yourself now at the core of the sun. Align with its pattern of function. Feel yourself being warmed and charged in its light and heat, which is of unspeakable magnitude. Without losing your own identity, you are blending into the sun. You are generating a million degrees of heat without being burned and a trillion amps of light without being blinded.

See the earth as being like a magnificent Christmas ornament hung in the sky. See where it can use your warmth and illumination, not just in a physical sense but in all ways. Spend a few minutes sending what is needed. When you feel complete, rematerialize your body at its former density or perhaps a little lighter, and return to the room.

NOTES

25 🌿 DISSOLVING BLOCKS

Find yourself being completely peaceful. Feel well-being coming from the deepest part of you, filling your entire being. The boundaries between you and the rest of life are softening. Your oneness with all is more and more apparent to you. Your mind is becoming still. You are experiencing this moment purely, without interference.

It is good to be alive, to be a part of all life! It is easy to be alive! Problems do not limit your aliveness or happiness. They are simply challenges that give you opportunities to make choices and grow. As you increasingly open to yourself, happiness wells up from deep inside you. Feel it.

The highest form of energy, love, now completely surrounds you and this room, dissolving blocks. Let yourself receive more and more love into yourself.

∽ NOTES ∾

26 ❦ THE MASTER

You are transported by thought to an ashram in the Himalayas. It is a pristine day. The air is sublime. It energizes and relaxes you at the same time.

A great master enters. He does not speak, but you know his thoughts. He begins to chant. You hear this chant inside of you only. Your body resonates with the chant. It moves to a higher and higher vibration. Continue to receive this chant within you for several minutes. When it is finished, slowly come back to the room.

NOTES

L et every cell of your body be bathed in healing warmth and light. Allow to well up from deep within you a great feeling of well-being. Bask in it. Absorb it. Experience it making your body happy. Feel a great peace enfolding you. Begin to sense a growing connectedness with everyone else on earth.

Now ask that your essence, your inner being, come forth. Receive it first at the crown of your head. Feel it slowly moving down your body, welcoming it into every point along the way.

When you are done, open your eyes and bring your consciousness back to the room, careful to maintain a welcome to the presence of your essence.

NOTES

28   ASCENSION

F eel a magnetic force directly above you, gently drawing you upward. It is as if in becoming relaxed, all the parts of your body release energetic substance, like the bubbles of champagne rising upwards.

As energy is drawn from you upward, you are also drawing energy into you from the earth below you. This earth energy makes you feel warm, grounded, and connected to the whole earth. Feel it coming into each cell of your body and continue to feel the energetic substance being drawn upward by the magnetic force above you.

When you feel completely balanced and energized, or when you otherwise feel complete, return to the room.

NOTES

29 ❧ AFFIRMATIONS

Y ou are becoming totally carefree. All your bur-
dens slide off your back, so that you feel as light
as a feather. A magical old crone comes by with
a large cart to collect all your troubles. They are food for
her, so you give generously, holding none back. She disappears into the horizon.

You are rich. Think of some of the ways that you
are rich, such as in the beauty of the earth and the people who love you. Let awareness of this abundance
penetrate your core.

Affirmations do not rightly cover over the challenges of life, but help you to see them from a place of
strength rather than weakness, to be the source of your
life rather than the victim of outside influences. Repeat
in your mind three times each of these affirmations, and
let yourself absorb the way that they feel:

All is well.
I am strong.
I can easily handle everything that happens.
I love life, and life loves me.
I am glad to be on earth.
I let myself be happy.
I let myself enjoy life and have fun.
I let myself be in peace.

Now, create a visualization of the feeling of freedom and
be with it for a few moments.

NOTES

30 ❧ RECHARGING

Visualize in your solar plexus a great rechargeable battery. See yourself as floating in the middle of the sun, which is the greatest source of energy known to you. Feel that battery receiving it and being charged up.

The battery is a round bluish-green globe, like the earth. As it absorbs energy from the sun, its color turns to that of the sun. When you can no longer see the globe but only the sun within and without, go through your body starting from your toes and visualize the sun energy being absorbed into your flesh.

NOTES

31 ❧ THE ISLAND

You are an airplane, solar-powered, silent, light, yet strong. You are soaring up through an azure-blue sky. As you ascend, you see more and more of the earth. You notice a magical island not on the map. It is lush and beautiful. Its buildings are constructed of translucent rock that seems to change color as you look at it from different angles. You effortlessly land, and you become this island. The people of this island are peaceful, loving, and wise. They evolve through joy rather than through pain and misery.

Spend some time being this island, getting to know it, and seeing what lessons it has for you. When you are ready, become the airplane again and fly home, seeing the earth beneath you in a new way, in recognition of its potential.

NOTES

32 ❧ LIFE FORCE

Feel your life force moving freely in you. Notice how it is moving in your body. Where is it the most free, and the least? Rejoice where you find it moving without obstruction. Where the life force is frozen, bring the warmth of your being to that place to help thaw what is not moving.

As life force moves more freely, your sense of well-being expands. Notice your sense of well-being. Give thanks for it. Your life force is now bringing you into oneness with all life force. When it is complete, enjoy being life force for as long as it feels appropriate. Then return your consciousness to your personal life force, and then to an awareness of the room.

NOTES

33   BEING

Allow yourself to be like air, floating suspended, carrier of hot and cold, light and dark, but beyond these things.

Allow yourself to be like fire, which cannot be burned because it is the flame, a bringer of warmth and light, transmuting matter into spirit.

Allow yourself to be like earth, infinitely strong yet delicate and beautiful, a bringer of life form, a Great Mother to all that lives, yet beyond form.

Allow yourself to be like water, which can easily take the shape of any vessel and yet not be limited by any vessel, leaking out through cracks, evaporating or overflowing, in total freedom.

Allow yourself to be like sound, which expresses itself and then is content to fade away, leaving no mark, yet forever changing the universe.

Allow yourself to be all things. Allow yourself to be no thing. Allow yourself to be.

NOTES

34 ❧ THE ANIMAL

Feel your entire body. When you will it, your body will be transformed into the body of any animal you choose. Select whatever animal comes first to your awareness, and feel yourself becoming that. Spend a few minutes being that, seeing what adventures and lessons you have.

When you are through, become again who you are, and discuss with your inner teacher what you learned.

NOTES

35 ❧ THE JOURNEY ANYWHERE

You are seated on a chair made of clouds. This chair is the most comfortable chair that you have ever sat in. It surrounds you and completely supports you. It begins to safely lift you off the ground, and you glide through the air as if in a space vehicle, going as slowly or as quickly as you wish, enjoying the view. Feel the delight of gliding through the air, freely and effortlessly, utterly silent.

Above you, Father Sun and Mother Moon are smiling warmly upon you. The sky is any way that you would like it to be: the deepest, clearest blue or the starriest, blackest night. You can use your imagination to create a rainbow sky or anything else that pleases you.

You are about to take a journey to any place you would like to go: a far planet or inside your own body, another plane or another place on earth. Let yourself go wherever you wish.

At the end of your journey, you will meet a friend who will help you understand the significance of it. When you are ready, come back to the room.

NOTES

36 ❧ SILENCE

Silence. Silence permeates the spaces between these words. As mortar fills in the spaces between bricks, silence fills the spaces between the cells of your body. Your cells bathe in silence. Each cell absorbs silence as a sponge absorbs clean, refreshing water.

In the silence, the cells can be heard. Listen to them. Let them empty their concerns into the silence, so that they may find peace. Do not engage in dialogue. Just listen. When your cells have said what they would say to you, enjoy the silence and peace together. When you are finished, return to the room.

NOTES

37 ❁ TRUTH

See before you a vision of truth. Not truth as concept, but truth manifested as beauty. This vision can take any form you wish. It can be a work of art, something from the natural world, or something you have never seen before.

Gaze upon whatever arises for you until you feel you are a part of it. Begin to walk through this vision. How does it change you? What from this living vision can you bring back with you into your life?

Your vision of truth is different from that of others, yet there is something in common among all visions of truth. Sense what that is. Again, avoid conceptualizing. Ask now that this common thread of truth lead you on an expansion of your vision. Let yourself experience being a part of other aspects of truth. When you are ready, return to the room.

NOTES

38 🌺 THE DARKNESS

Often we meditate on the Light. The Light is beautiful. The darkness is also beautiful. It is in the dark night sky that you can see the stars and the moon. In the womb, it is dark and safe, a place in which what is new can take form. Darkness enfolds us, just as light does.

Visualize yourself surrounded by rich, black, velvety darkness. Feel yourself to be completely safe in the darkness. Out of this sacred darkness you hear a voice. It is the voice of one who is dear to you. Hear what this voice tells you. Receive it and remember it.

The darkness has beautiful variations, just as the light does. See the movement of deep, rich, dark, powerful colors: purples, violets, maroons, and browns. See their glorious nighttime patterns all around you. Blend into them. Move with them. Lose any sense of self apart from these movements of sensuous forces.

Know the real meaning of darkness. It is not evil. It is creative possibility, that which receives, the feminine principle of being.

As darkness, begin to welcome light into yourself in whatever form pleases you, maybe as one ray of light from a celestial body, maybe as a sun coming forth from within you, as though you were giving birth to it. You may wish to ride this light like a child might imagine himself riding a meteorite. Experience oneness with the light as darkness. Feel the wholeness that brings. Be with that wholeness until you are ready to return to the room.

❧ NOTES ☙

39 ❧ THE OCEAN

Feel your whole being transforming itself into a form that can go anywhere. You are now at the ocean. As you gaze upon it, you become it. Experience yourself as being the ocean. What are you like on your ocean floor? What are your waves like? Feel how deep you are and how far you stretch in all directions.

You contain many forms of life. Survey those forms of life. Some are quite large, some are microscopic. Choose one of them, and in any way you wish, get to know it quite well. When you have completed this, return to your human form.

NOTES

40 HEART

Your heart is not merely an organ, limited in its size and shape. It is at your core between your inner and outer selves. Become aware of your heart as it springs from the place of your physical heart. Feel it expanding until it creates a sphere several feet beyond the confines of your skin. Feel that heart substance bathing you, filling you to overflowing with joy and a sense of goodness. Feel the safety of dwelling within this great heart.

The heart is a place of integration. Ask your heart to show you something in you that can be integrated now, something that is ready to come into light and be healed with love. Your heart can show you in thought, sound, sensation, or in any other way. Be with whatever is given and let the process begin. You do not have to make it happen; simply let it. Move in this way as long as the process carries you along. When you are ready, open your eyes, trusting that the integration will continue until it is complete.

NOTES

41 ❧ ALIVENESS

Feel the aliveness of your body. Be at the source of that aliveness. Now sense those elements in you that are afraid of being too alive. Be with them until their energies dissipate. Then feel your aliveness increase to its maximum potential. When you are done, simply enjoy your aliveness.

NOTES

42 ❧ SOUL FLIGHT

et relaxation come to every part of your body. It pours in like a healing elixir. A gong sounds. Your whole being resonates with it. Wind chimes make music. The gentle peace of sunset is with you. Its pink, blue, and yellow colors soothe you. A soft breeze carries the fragrance of flowering trees.

Your soul begins to lift up out of your body. From a high place, you survey the magnificent scene. While your body is being rejuvenated, your soul is free to do anything that it wishes. Be with your soul, and let it take you where it will. When you are done, return to your body, and gradually bring your consciousness back to the room.

NOTES

43 ❧ THE LIGHTFALL

Picture yourself standing beneath a waterfall of light. It is soothing and healing you. You find it to be completely relaxing and invigorating at the same time. Feel every cell in your body giving way under the pressure of this "lightfall." Stay with it until your body becomes the light.

NOTES

44 ❧ THE GREAT TREE

The night's rich blackness enfolds you. The vivid moon illuminates your path. The Milky Way is a shimmering canopy under which you walk protected. Your heart leaps for joy at the beauty of this night. The trees and bushes speak to you differently than in the intensity of day. Their inner selves are more exposed.

You are standing before a great being, a towering tree. It invites you into itself, and you go. Allow him to show you his treasures. When you are both done, return to an awareness of this room.

❧

NOTES

45 ❧ THE FUTURE

See yourself in the middle of a forest. You are walking slowly down a beautiful path through it. It is a beautiful, warm August morning. A squirrel approaches you and you stop. You pick him up and pet him like a kitten. Then you put him down and continue on your way. He joins you as your guide.

He leads you into a secret cave. You sit on a rock until your eyes become accustomed to the light. This cave is known as "The Cave of the Future." As you walk through it, you are shown the direction of your present course and where it is leading you. Follow the squirrel and see what the cave shows you.

This cave has many different paths through it. If you are not pleased with what you are first shown, you can ask the squirrel to show you an alternative path, a different future based on changing your direction. When you are done, go back into the forest, and then return to the room.

NOTES

ABOUT THE AUTHOR

Shepherd Hoodwin is a New York City channel and teacher, workshop leader, counselor, and channeling coach. He has been channeling his essence and Michael since 1986. He is the author of several articles on the Michael teachings and six books of channeled material, including *The Journey of Your Soul—A Channel Explores Channeling and the Michael Teachings* and *Loving from Your Soul—Creating Powerful Relationships.*. He is a graduate of the University of Oregon in Music Education, and is a songwriter, singer, and actor. He is currently writing a musical.

To write to Shepherd, or to obtain information about his workshops, private sessions, Michael Readings, and about other Summerjoy Press books and cassettes, write Summerjoy Press, FDR Station Box 7590, New York NY 10150-1913. You can order Summerjoy Press books through any bookstore, or from Atrium Publishers Group, 1-800-275-2606. Volume discounts for individuals are available from the publisher.

ACKNOWLEDGMENTS

Leslie-Anne Skolnik, Linda Scheurle, Seth Cohn, Fay Goldie, Kent Babcock, Barry Carl, Pat Kendall, Evelyn Jones, Billy Jim, Richard Reed, Sylvia Dweck, Mayo Gray, Neil Rubenstein, and Flo Nakamura.